This Book Belongs to

_____

This book is dedicated to my grandson, Grayson- lover of goggles, gizmos, and gadgets!

Grayson James absolutely loves to wear his green goggles. They are the first thing he puts on each morning and the last thing he takes off each night. He would sleep in them but his mother says goggles and pajamas do not go together. That's why he caused such a commotion when he could not find them one morning.

"Mom, I can't find my goggles anywhere," Grayson hollers.

"Help! They're gone!" he screams.

"Calm down," she replies, "and I'll come help you find them."

"But Mom, I have to wear my goggles or I can't be G-Man and they aren't in my room!" he gasps, panic in his voice.

Grayson's mother calmly walks into his room and begins searching through his toy box, his closet, his dresser drawers, and under his bed. Grayson is right -- the goggles have disappeared!

"Let's look in the garage" mom suggests. "You were wearing them yesterday and probably just left them on the car seat."

Grayson runs as fast as he can to the garage, looks in the car, and groans, "Oh no, they aren't in the car! Where can they be? What shall we do?"

Mother tells him they should stop and think about all the places they visited yesterday. "We can retrace our steps," she says. "I'll take you back to each one and we can search for the goggles. Do you remember where we went first?"

"The zoo," he grins, "I bet I left them at the zoo."

They dress quickly and return to the zoo. "I remember visiting the gazelles, the gorillas, the grizzly bears, and the giraffes," Grayson reminds her. "I thought the gazelles were grand, the gorillas were a little grumpy, but the giraffes were very gentle."

"What a great gift of gab you have," Mom smiles. They return to each area and search all around, but do not find the goggles.

"Ok, where did we go next?" Mom wonders.

"Let me think," Grayson says as he lowers his head and closes his eyes, "we went to the grocery store!"

They return to the grocery store and search every aisle where they had purchased grapefruit, gherkins, goji berries, gingersnaps, graham crackers, granola, ginger ale, and guacamole.

"Don't forget we bought some grape jelly!" Grayson gasps, "That's G-Man's favorite!"

But no goggles were to be found.

"What was our next stop?" Mom asks.

"We went to the farm, " he replies.

"Let's go back there!"

They drive to the farm and carefully examine the ground around the goat pen and the areas where they observed some grouse and gophers.

"Maybe I left them when we fed the geese and the baby gosling," Grayson says. "Remember how I giggled because you said a gaggle of geese were looking at my goggles?"

Sadly, they were not there.

"I could have lost them when I was chasing the grasshoppers," he thinks. But they could not find the goggles anywhere.

"We walked through the gardens where vegetables and fruits were growing. Let's look there again," Grayson urges.

They check out the rows of gooseberry bushes, green pepper plants, garbanzo beans, garlic, ginger, and gourds. Sorrowfully, the goggles are not found, but they see some geraniums germinating in the flower garden.

"Didn't we stop by the garbage dump so I could look for some gadgets?" he asks. Let's stop there next.

At the garbage dump they don't find his goggles, but they do pick up two old gyroscopes, an old generator, and some greasy looking gizmos Grayson thought he could use.

"Where did we go next?" mother asks.

"We stopped by the gymnasium so you could exercise," he responds.

"We had to walk through some gravel and I bet they fell off then."

Hurrying back to the gym, they see a golf cart, a gymnast carrying a gunnysack, and a group of guys playing guitars. They do not see any goggles.

"I remember stopping in the park for a few minutes on the way to the pet store. Let's look there."

They walk through the grassy areas of the park and see a German Shepherd and a Golden Retriever playing frisbee with their owners. They also see a Great Dane and a gray Greyhound fetching tennis balls, but once again, they cannot find the goggles.

Finally, Mother said they had to give up. The goggles were lost. They would go to the mall and try to find him another pair.

Grayson grumbles, "but I really loved those gigantic green goggles. What if we can't find any more in the entire galaxy like them?"

"We will keep looking until we do," mother promises.

"Let's stop by grandmothers house before we go home" says Mom.

When they walk into the kitchen, there's Gammy, eating a bowl of goulash with grits. But best of all, she is wearing Grayson's gigantic green goggles!!

"Look what I found," she exclaims, as she reaches for the precious goggles and hands them back. Grayson gulps as he remembers taking them off to help Gammy glue gumdrops on the gingerbread cookies they made. His goggles have been here all the time.

"Thanks for taking such good care of them for me," he gushes. "I love my goggles, but I love you more!"

"How gallant of you, G-Man," Gammy guffaws, "but I love you most!"

Glossary

Gadgets -- any object that is interesting for its ingenuity or novelty rather than for its practical use

Gaggle -- a flock of geese when not flying

Galaxy -- a massive interstellar system consisting of stars, gas, and dust

Gallant -- courteous, polite, mannerly, considerate, and thoughtful

Garbanzo beans -- a legume also known as a chickpea, loaded with protein and fiber

Gazelles -- small antelope noted for graceful movements

Generator -- a machine that converts one form of energy into another

Geraniums -- flowers with fragrant leaves, vivid red color

German Shepherd -- one of a breed of large shepherd dogs having a coat ranging in color from gray to brindled, black-and-tan, or black, used especially in police work and as a guide for the blind

Germinating -- to begin to grow or develop into a plant

Gherkins -- a small pickle

Gingersnaps -- a small, brittle cookie flavored with ginger and molasses

Gizmos -- slang for a device or a gadget

Goggles -- large spectacles equipped with special lenses to prevent injury to the eyes from strong wind, flying objects, blinding light, etc.

Goji berries -- shriveled red berries that look like raisins

Golden Retriever -- a compact large breed of dog having a silky coat of flat or wavy hair of a gold or dark-cream color, well-feathered on the legs and tail

Gooseberry -- a shrub having greenish, purple-tinged flowers and red-purple berries

Gorillas -- the largest of the apes

Gosling -- a young goose

Goulash -- a rich stew of beef or veal with vegetables, seasoned with paprika

Gourds -- a hard shelled fruit whose dried shell is used for bowls and other utensils

Granola -- a mixture of rolled oats, brown sugar, nuts, and dried fruit

Great Dane -- a very large powerful yet graceful breed of dog with a short smooth coat

Greyhound -- a tall slender short-haired dog, noted for its keen sight and swiftness

Grits -- coarsely ground hominy, boiled and eaten as a breakfast or side dish

Grouse -- a popular game bird having a pulp body and feathered legs and feet

Guffaws -- to laugh loudly and boisterously

Guinea Pigs -- a short-eared, tailless rodent, often kept as a pet

Gunnysack -- a sack or bag made of burlap

Gyroscopes -- a device consisting of a rotating wheel mounted so that it can turn freely on its axis in all directions; used to determine direction

Gymnasium -- a building or room designed for indoor sports or exercise

Gymnast -- a person trained and skilled in gymnastics

www.ingramcontent.com/pod-product-compliance
Lightning Source LLC
Chambersburg PA
CBHW051554010526
44118CB00022B/2707